RETIRE

with

CONFIDENCE

*A Comprehensive Guide to Financial
Security and Fulfillment*

JEFFREY FERON

TABLE OF CONTENT

Retire with Confidence

INTRODUCTION

Sarah was a determined soul with dreams as vast as the horizon. From her early days, she understood the value of hard work and perseverance.

Starting as a young intern at a bustling financial firm, she absorbed knowledge like a sponge, eager to learn the ropes of the trade. As the years flew by, Sarah climbed the corporate ladder, each rung a testament to her dedication and resilience.

Her secret? Sarah wasn't just accumulating a paycheck; she was building a future. Every bonus, every raise, and every investment she made wasn't just about wealth accumulation; it was a step towards her goal of retiring with not just financial security, but also with fulfillment.

Sarah didn't just focus on amassing wealth; she understood the importance of balance. She volunteered, traveled, nurtured hobbies, and cultivated meaningful relationships along the way. Her retirement fund wasn't just numbers on a statement; it was a testament to her life's work, a culmination of sacrifices and wise choices.

When the time finally came for Sarah to bid farewell to the corporate world, she did so with a sense of accomplishment. She had meticulously planned for this moment, envisioning a life filled with purpose and joy beyond the confines of her office.

Retirement wasn't an end for Sarah; it was a new chapter. Armed with financial security and a heart full of passions, she embraced this phase of life with enthusiasm. She mentored youngsters, explored new interests, traveled to far-off lands, and cherished the moments spent with loved ones.

Her story became an inspiration—an embodiment of what it meant to retire with confidence. Not just financially secure, but emotionally fulfilled and spiritually content. People sought her advice, not just on financial matters, but on life's journey as a whole.

Sarah's journey wasn't without challenges, setbacks, or doubts. Yet, her unwavering determination and careful planning guided her through the storms. Her story echoed the essence of retiring with confidence—a fusion of financial stability, personal fulfillment, and a life well-lived.

Welcome to "Retire with Confidence: A Comprehensive Guide to Financial Security and Fulfillment." In this book, we will embark on a journey of retirement planning, equipping you with the knowledge and tools necessary to navigate this significant life transition successfully.

Retirement is not just about financial security; it is about finding fulfillment, purpose, and joy in this new chapter of your life. Whether you are just starting to think about retirement or are already on the cusp of this milestone, this guide will provide you with valuable insights and practical advice to help you retire with confidence.

"As the sun sets on your career, let the glow of financial wisdom light the way to a radiant retirement."

Anonymous

   Retire with Confidence

1

THE IMPORTANCE OF RETIREMENT PLANNING

Retirement Planning is often overlooked or delayed due to various reasons. Many individuals believe that retirement is far into the future and that they have plenty of time to save and prepare.

However, the truth is that time flies, and before you know it, retirement is just around the corner. It is essential to recognize the significance of retirement planning and the potential consequences of neglecting it.

In this chapter, we will explore the importance of retirement planning and the benefits it brings. Retirement planning provides a sense of security and peace of mind, knowing that you have taken the necessary steps to ensure a comfortable future. It allows you to make informed decisions about your finances, lifestyle, and overall well-being.

One of the primary reasons retirement planning is crucial is the uncertainty surrounding government benefits and social security. While these programs provide a safety net, they may not be sufficient to meet all your needs during retirement. By planning ahead, you can bridge the gap and ensure that you have enough financial resources to support your desired lifestyle.

Additionally, retirement planning allows you to set realistic goals and establish a roadmap to achieve them. It helps you identify your desired retirement age, income requirements, and lifestyle preferences. By having a clear vision of your retirement, you can align your financial decisions and actions accordingly.

Furthermore, retirement planning provides an opportunity to evaluate your current financial situation. It allows you to assess your assets, liabilities, income, and expenses. This assessment helps you identify areas for improvement and make necessary adjustments to achieve your retirement goals.

Another advantage of retirement planning is the potential for tax savings. By strategically managing your investments and retirement accounts, you can minimize your tax obligations and maximize your savings. Understanding the tax implications of different retirement strategies can significantly impact your long-term financial security.

Moreover, retirement planning promotes financial discipline and responsible money management. It encourages you to save consistently, invest wisely, and avoid unnecessary debt. By developing good financial habits early on, you can build a strong foundation for a secure retirement.

Lastly, retirement planning is not solely about finances. It is about envisioning your ideal retirement lifestyle and taking steps to achieve it. It involves considering factors such as healthcare, leisure activities, travel, and personal fulfillment. By planning for these aspects, you can create a retirement that is truly fulfilling and meaningful.

In summary, retirement planning is of utmost importance for several key reasons. It provides financial security, allows you to set goals and create a roadmap, evaluates your current financial situation, offers potential tax savings, promotes financial discipline, and helps you envision and achieve a fulfilling retirement lifestyle.

As we dive deeper into this comprehensive guide, we will explore each of these aspects in greater detail. You will gain valuable insights, practical tips, and actionable steps to ensure that you retire with confidence, financial security, and a sense of fulfillment.

Remember, it is never too late or too early to begin planning for your retirement. So, let's embark on this journey together and pave the way to a secure and fulfilling retirement.

"A retirement well-earned is a testament to a lifetime of thoughtful financial decisions."

Anonymous

2

ASSESSING YOUR RETIREMENT NEEDS

Now that we understand the importance of retirement planning, it's time to delve into the process of assessing your retirement needs. This chapter will guide you through the essential considerations when determining how much money you will require during your retirement years.

1. Current Expenses: Begin by evaluating your current expenses. Take a close look at your monthly spending habits, including necessities such as housing, food, transportation, healthcare, and utilities. Consider any discretionary expenses, such as travel or hobbies that you may want to continue during retirement.

2. Inflation: Keep in mind that the cost of living will likely increase over time due to inflation. Estimate the rate of inflation and factor it into your retirement calculations. This will ensure that your projected expenses are realistic and account for future price increases.

     Retire with Confidence

3. Lifestyle Goals: Consider the lifestyle you envision for your retirement. Do you plan to travel extensively, pursue expensive hobbies, or downsize to a simpler lifestyle? These choices will impact your financial needs. Be realistic about your expectations and determine how much additional income you may require to support your desired lifestyle.

4. Healthcare Costs: Healthcare expenses tend to rise as we age. Research the costs of health insurance, Medicare, and long-term care insurance. Consider potential out-of-pocket expenses for prescription medications, doctor visits, and any specific health conditions you may have. It's important to account for these costs in your plan for retirement.

5. Social Security: Understand how Social Security benefits will contribute to your retirement income. Determine the age at which you plan to start receiving benefits and calculate the estimated amount you will receive. Keep in mind that delaying your benefits can result in higher monthly payments, so weigh the pros and cons of timing your Social Security withdrawals.

6. Pension and Retirement Accounts: If you have a pension or retirement accounts, evaluate the projected income they will provide during retirement. Consider consulting with a financial advisor to assess the best strategies for maximizing your retirement savings and optimizing withdrawals.

7. Life Expectancy: While none of us can predict the future, estimating your life expectancy can help gauge the duration of your retirement years. Consider your family history, lifestyle factors, and overall health. Planning for a longer life expectancy ensures that you

   Retire with Confidence

have sufficient funds to support yourself throughout your retirement.

8. Additional Income Sources: Explore potential additional income sources, such as rental properties, part-time work, or side businesses. These can supplement your retirement savings and provide a safety net in case of unexpected expenses or market fluctuations.

9. Review and Adjust: Remember that retirement planning is an ongoing process. Regularly review and make adjustments to your retirement plan as circumstances change. Life events, market conditions, and personal goals may require you to revisit and revise your financial strategy.

By carefully assessing your retirement needs, you can create a realistic financial plan that accounts for your desired lifestyle, healthcare costs, and potential income sources. Take the time to gather accurate information, consult with professionals if needed, and be proactive in shaping your retirement future.

In the next chapter, we will explore different investment strategies to help you grow your retirement savings effectively. Stay tuned as we continue this journey toward a secure and fulfilling retirement.

> *"The wise retiree doesn't just look back on their career; they look forward to a retirement shaped by foresight." - Unknown*

3

INVESTMENT STRATEGIES FOR RETIREMENT PLANNING

Now that we have assessed your retirement needs, it's time to explore effective investment strategies that can help grow your retirement savings. In this chapter, we will discuss various investment options to consider as you plan for your future.

1. Diversification: Diversifying your investment portfolio is crucial for mitigating risk and maximizing returns. Ensure you Spread your investments across different classes of assets such as stocks, real estate, bonds, and mutual funds. This diversification helps balance potential gains and losses, ensuring a more stable and sustainable retirement income.

2. Stocks: Investing in stocks can provide long-term growth potential. While stocks can be volatile, they historically offer higher returns compared to other investment options. Consider investing in a diversified mix of large-cap, mid-cap, and small-cap stocks to spread risk and capture market opportunities.

 Retire with Confidence

3. Bonds: Bonds are considered safer investments that provide income through interest payments. Corporate bonds, municipal bonds and Government bonds are common options. Bonds offer stability and can be a valuable addition to your retirement portfolio, especially for those seeking a more conservative approach.

4. Mutual Funds: Mutual funds creates an avenue to pool money from multiple investors to invest in a diverse portfolio of stocks, bonds, or other assets. They are professionally managed, making them a convenient option for those who prefer a hands-off approach. Mutual funds offer diversification and can be tailored to align with your risk tolerance and investment goals.

5. Exchange-Traded Funds (ETFs) operate akin to mutual funds; however, they are traded on stock exchanges like individual stocks. They offer diversification, lower expense ratios, and the flexibility to buy and sell throughout the trading day. ETFs are popular among investors looking for cost-effective and convenient investment options.

6. Real Estate: Real estate can be a valuable addition to your retirement portfolio. Consider investing in real estate investment trusts (REITs), real estate crowdfunding platforms or rental properties. Real estate investments can provide consistent income through rental payments and potential appreciation over time.

7. Retirement Accounts: Maximize your contributions to retirement accounts such as 401(k)s, IRAs, and Roth IRAs. These accounts provide tax benefits and can substantially enhance your retirement savings. Take advantage of employer matching contributions, if

available, and consider automating contributions to ensure consistent saving.

8. Annuities: Annuities are insurance products that provide regular income payments during retirement. They offer a guaranteed income stream, which can be appealing for those seeking stability. However, it's important to carefully evaluate the terms, fees, and potential limitations of annuities before making a decision.

9. Seek Professional Guidance: Contemplate engaging with a financial advisor with expertise in retirement planning. They can offer tailored advice tailored to your specific circumstances, risk tolerance, and objectives. A professional can help create a customized investment strategy that aligns with your retirement needs.

10. Regular Monitoring and Rebalancing: Continuously monitor your investment portfolio and make adjustments as needed. Periodically adjust your portfolio to uphold the desired asset allocation. Market conditions, economic factors, and your changing risk tolerance may require adjustments to ensure your investments align with your retirement goals.

Remember, investing for retirement is a long-term commitment. It's important to stay informed, be patient, and make decisions based on your circumstances. By diversifying your portfolio, leveraging different investment options, and seeking professional advice when needed, you can position yourself for a financially secure retirement.

In the next chapter, we will discuss strategies to optimize your Social Security benefits and make the most of this valuable retirement resource. Stay tuned as we continue our journey toward a fulfilling retirement.

"In the book of life, the chapter on retirement is written with the ink of wisdom and the pen of preparation." - Anonymous

4

MAXIMIZING YOUR SOCIAL SECURITY BENEFITS

For many individuals, Social Security benefits play a significant role in their retirement income. In this chapter, we will explore strategies to optimize your Social Security benefits and make the most of this valuable resource.

1. Understand Your Eligibility: Familiarize yourself with the eligibility requirements for Social Security benefits. Generally, you need to have earned a certain number of credits through employment to qualify. Keep track of your earnings history to ensure accuracy when calculating your benefits.

2. Determine the Best Age to Claim: You can start receiving Social Security benefits as early as age 62, but your monthly payments will be reduced. On the other hand, if you delay claiming benefits beyond your full retirement age (typically between 66 and 67, depending on your birth year), your monthly payments will increase. Consider your financial situation, health, and longevity expectations when deciding the optimal age to claim.

    Retire with Confidence

3. Consider Spousal Benefits: If you are married or divorced but were married for at least ten years, you may be eligible for spousal benefits based on your spouse's earnings record. Spousal benefits can provide an additional source of income during retirement. Explore the options and potential advantages of claiming spousal benefits.

4. Coordinate with Your Spouse: If both you and your spouse are eligible for Social Security benefits, strategize on how to maximize your combined benefits. Depending on your individual earnings histories, it may be beneficial for one spouse to claim benefits earlier while the other delays, allowing for larger cumulative payments over time.

5. Understand the Earnings Test: If you choose to claim Social Security benefits before your full retirement age and continue working, your benefits may be reduced if your earnings exceed a certain threshold. Familiarize yourself with the earnings test rules to make informed decisions regarding the timing of your benefit claims.

6. Consider Tax Implications: A portion of your Social Security benefits may be subject to federal income taxes, depending on your overall income. Understand the tax rules and implications to effectively plan for your retirement income and potential tax obligations.

7. Factor in Survivor Benefits: Social Security provides survivor benefits to eligible widows, widowers, and dependents of deceased beneficiaries. Understanding the potential survivor benefits can help

 Retire with Confidence

you make decisions that maximize financial security for your loved ones after your passing.

8. Utilize Online Tools and Resources: The Social Security Administration offers various online tools and resources to help you calculate and estimate your benefits. Take advantage of these tools to explore different claiming scenarios and make informed decisions about your retirement income strategy.

9. Investigate State Specifics: Recognize that Social Security benefits can be subject to state taxes in certain locations. Investigate the tax implications in your state and consider the potential impact on your overall retirement income. Relocating strategically could positively affect your tax situation.

9. Seek Professional Advice: Social Security rules and strategies can be complex. The key to maximizing Social Security benefits is a personalized approach. Evaluate your unique circumstances, consider your long-term goals, and, if needed, consult with a financial advisor to create a strategy tailored to your retirement

> *"The wise retiree builds a financial fortress, understanding that peace of mind is the best retirement asset." - Unknown*

5

THE IMPORTANCE OF HEALTHY LIVING IN RETIREMENT

Retirement is a time to enjoy the fruits of your labor and embrace a new chapter in life. In this chapter, we will explore the importance of maintaining a healthy lifestyle during retirement and how it can positively impact your overall well-being.

1. Physical Health: Engaging in regular physical activity is crucial for maintaining good health in retirement. Incorporate activities such as walking, swimming, yoga, or strength training into your routine. Physical exercise not only improves cardiovascular health and strength but also helps manage weight, reduce the risk of chronic diseases, and enhance overall mobility and flexibility.

2. Mental Stimulation: Keep your mind sharp and engaged by participating in mentally stimulating activities. Read books, solve puzzles, play strategy games, or take up a new hobby that challenges your cognitive abilities. Engaging in intellectually stimulating activities can help prevent cognitive decline and promote mental well-being.

3. Nutritious Diet: Pay attention to your diet and opt for a well-balanced and nutritious eating plan.Incorporate a diverse range of fruits, vegetables, whole grains, lean proteins, and healthy fats into your meals. A healthy diet can provide the necessary nutrients for optimal physical and mental health, boost your immune system, and decrease the risk of chronic diseases.

4. Social Connections: Stay socially active and maintain strong relationships with family and friends. Participate in social gatherings, join clubs or community organizations, or volunteer for causes that are meaningful to you. Social connections contribute to emotional well-being, provide a support system, and combat feelings of isolation or loneliness.

5. Sleep and Relaxation: Prioritize quality sleep and relaxation. Set up a consistent sleep routine and design an environment conducive to sleep. Practice relaxation techniques such as meditation, deep breathing exercises, or engaging in activities that help you unwind. Sufficient rest and relaxation are essential for physical and mental rejuvenation.

6. Preventive Healthcare: Regular preventive healthcare check-ups are vital for monitoring your health and detecting any potential issues early on. Schedule routine visits with your healthcare provider, undergo recommended screenings, and follow their guidance for preventive measures such as vaccinations, screenings, and health maintenance.

7. Stress Management: Retirement can bring its own set of stressors, such as financial concerns or adjusting to a new routine. Implement stress management techniques such as mindfulness, meditation, or

 Retire with Confidence

engaging in activities that bring you joy and relaxation. Managing stress effectively can improve overall well-being and reduce the risk of stress-related health conditions.

8. Purpose and Meaning: Find activities or pursuits that give you a sense of purpose and meaning in retirement. Explore volunteer opportunities, mentorship programs, or engage in hobbies that bring fulfillment and a sense of accomplishment. Having a sense of purpose can improve mental health, enhance self-esteem, and provide a structure to your days.

9. Emotional Well-being: Pay attention to your emotional well-being and seek support if needed. Retirement can bring about emotional changes, such as adjusting to a new identity or navigating a sense of loss. Reach out to a therapist, counselor, or support group to help process these emotions and maintain a healthy emotional balance.

10. Balance and Enjoyment: Finally, remember to strike a balance between taking care of your health and enjoying the freedom and relaxation that retirement brings. Embrace leisure activities, travel, pursue hobbies, and spend quality time with loved ones. Retirement is a time to savor the joys of life, so make sure to prioritize self-care and enjoyment.

By prioritizing your health and well-being during retirement, you can enhance your overall quality of life and make the most of this new chapter. Implementing healthy habits and seeking support when needed can contribute to a fulfilling and vibrant retirement journey.

In the next chapter, we will delve into the topic of legacy planning and how to leave a lasting impact through thoughtful estate planning. Join us as we continue our journey toward a fulfilling retirement.

> *"Planning for the future, even in the twilight of one's career, is the mark of a wise individual."*
> *- Anonymous*

6

CRAFTING YOUR LEGACY: A GUIDE TO ESTATE PLANNING

As we journey through retirement, it's essential to consider how we want to leave a lasting impact on the world. In this chapter, we will explore the importance of estate planning and how you can craft your legacy through thoughtful preparation.

1. Understand the Basics: Estate planning involves creating a comprehensive plan for the distribution of your assets and the management of your affairs after your passing. It includes elements such as drafting a will, establishing trusts, desiing beneficiaries, and making important healthcare and financial decisions.

2. Start Early: It's never too early to begin the estate planning process. By starting early, you have more time to carefully consider your wishes, gather necessary documents, and make any necessary adjustments as life circumstances change.

3. Identify Your Goals: Begin by clarifying your goals and priorities for your estate. Do you want to provide for your loved ones, support charitable causes, or leave a legacy for future generations?

     Retire with Confidence

Understanding your goals will guide the decisions you make throughout the estate planning process.

4. Create a Will: A will is a legal document that outlines how you want your assets to be distributed after your passing. It provides clear instructions and helps prevent confusion or disputes among your beneficiaries. Consult with an estate planning attorney to draft a will that reflects your wishes and meets legal requirements.

5. Establish Trusts: Trusts can be effective tools for managing and distributing your assets. They permit you to determine the method and timing for allocating your assets to your chosen beneficiaries. Explore different types of trusts, such as revocable living trusts or charitable trusts, to determine which best aligns with your goals.

6. Designate Beneficiaries: Review and update beneficiary designations on your various accounts, such as retirement plans, life insurance policies, and investment accounts. Make sure your chosen beneficiaries are current and align with your present preferences.

7. Plan for Incapacity: Estate planning isn't just about distributing assets after death; it also involves planning for potential incapacity. Consider creating powers of attorney for healthcare and financial matters, as well as advanced healthcare directives, to ensure your wishes are upheld if you're unable to make decisions for yourself.

8. Minimize Tax Impact: Understand the tax implications of your estate plan and explore strategies to minimize tax liabilities. Consult with a knowledgeable estate planning attorney or financial advisor

to explore options such as gifting, charitable giving, or establishing trusts that can help reduce the tax burden on your estate.

9. Communicate with Loved Ones: Openly discuss your estate plan with your loved ones. While it may be a sensitive topic, clear communication can help prevent misunderstandings and mitigate potential conflicts among family members. Share your intentions and explain the reasoning behind your decisions to promote understanding and harmony.

10. Regularly Review and Update: Estate planning is not a one-time event. As life evolves, it's vital to periodically reassess and revise your estate plan. Marriage, divorce, birth of children or grandchildren, changes in financial circumstances, or shifts in personal priorities may necessitate adjustments to your plan.

11. Consult Professionals: Estate planning can be complex, and it's advisable to seek guidance from professionals who specialize in this area. Consult with an experienced estate planning attorney, financial advisor, or tax professional who can provide valuable insights and ensure that your estate plan is comprehensive and aligned with your goals.

Crafting your legacy through estate planning allows you to leave a lasting impact on the people and causes you care about. By taking the time to plan thoughtfully, you can ensure that your wishes are fulfilled and provide peace of mind for yourself and your loved ones.

> *"Craft your retirement nest egg with the patience of a sculptor, creating a masterpiece for your golden years." - Anonymous*

7

EMBRACING LIFELONG LEARNING

Retirement offers a unique opportunity to invest in personal growth and expand our knowledge. In this chapter, we will explore the importance of lifelong learning and how it can enrich our lives during retirement.

1. Stimulate Your Mind: Engaging in lifelong learning keeps our minds active and sharp. It stimulates curiosity, enhances cognitive abilities, and promotes brain health. Embrace a growth mindset and approach each day as an opportunity to learn something new.

2. Pursue Formal Education: Consider enrolling in courses or pursuing a degree in a subject that interests you. Many universities and colleges offer programs specifically designed for retirees, providing a vibrant learning environment and the chance to interact with people of various ages and backgrounds.

3. Explore Online Learning: Take advantage of the wealth of knowledge available online. Platforms such as Coursera, edX, and Khan Academy offer a wide range of online courses taught by

    Retire with Confidence

experts in various fields. Dive into topics that intrigue you, whether it's history, science, art, or philosophy.

4. Join Study Groups: Seek out study groups or book clubs in your community that focus on intellectual discussions and shared learning experiences. Engaging with others who share similar interests can deepen your understanding of a subject and provide a sense of community.

5. Read Widely: Make reading a regular part of your routine. Discover various genres, authors, and topics to expand your perspectives. Visit your local library or join a book club to discover new perspectives and engage in meaningful discussions.

6. Attend Lectures and Workshops: Keep an eye out for lectures, workshops, and seminars in your area. Universities, museums, and community organizations often host these events, featuring renowned speakers and experts who can inspire and educate you on a wide range of topics.

7. Embrace New Technologies: Technology can be a powerful tool for learning. Explore online tutorials, webinars, and podcasts to expand your knowledge. Embrace new technologies such as e-readers or audiobooks to make learning more accessible and enjoyable.

8. Travel with a Purpose: Plan trips to destinations that offer opportunities for cultural immersion and learning. Visit museums, historical sites, and art galleries to gain insights into different

cultures and time periods. Engage with locals and learn about their traditions and customs.

9. Teach and Mentor Others: Share your knowledge and experiences with others by teaching or mentoring. Consider volunteering as a tutor or mentor for students or participating in community education programs. Teaching not only helps others but also reinforces your own understanding of a subject.

10. Engage in Creative Pursuits: Explore creative outlets such as painting, writing, music, or crafts. Engaging in creative activities stimulates the brain, fosters self-expression, and allows for personal growth and exploration.

11. Stay Curious: Cultivate a sense of curiosity and wonder about the world around you. Ask questions, seek answers, and never stop exploring. Embrace new ideas and challenge your own beliefs to foster intellectual growth and personal development.

Lifelong learning is a journey that never ends. By embracing intellectual growth during retirement, you can continue to expand your horizons, discover new passions, and maintain a vibrant and fulfilled life.

"In the book of life, the chapter on retirement is written with the ink of wisdom and the pen of preparation." - Anonymous

8

CULTIVATING MEANINGFUL CONNECTIONS

Retirement is not just a time for personal growth but also an opportunity to cultivate meaningful connections with others. In this chapter, we will explore the importance of maintaining a healthy and fulfilling social life during retirement.

1. Prioritize Relationships: Relationships are the foundation of a fulfilling social life. Prioritize nurturing existing relationships with family, friends, and loved ones. Make time for meaningful conversations, shared experiences, and create lasting memories together.

2. Join Social Clubs and Organizations: Seek out social clubs and organizations that align with your interests and passions. Whether it's a sports club, a book club, or a volunteer group, participating in these activities provides opportunities to connect with like-minded individuals and build new friendships.

3. Volunteer for a Cause: Giving back to the community through volunteering not only benefits others but also creates a sense of purpose and fulfillment in your own life. Identify causes or organizations that resonate with you and offer your time and skills to make a positive impact.

4. Attend Community Events: Stay involved in your community by attending local events, festivals, and gatherings. These events not only provide entertainment but also serve as platforms for socializing and connecting with fellow community members.

5. Embrace Technology for Social Connectivity: Leverage the power of technology to stay connected with friends and family, especially those who may be geographically distant. Utilize video calls, social media, and messaging platforms to maintain regular communication and share experiences.

6. Participate in Group Activities: Engage in group activities that promote social interaction and collaboration. This could include joining a sports team, participating in a choir or band, or taking part in group fitness classes. These activities foster a sense of belonging and camaraderie.

7. Attend Lifelong Learning Classes: As mentioned in the previous chapter, attending lifelong learning classes not only stimulates your mind but also provides opportunities to meet new people with similar interests. Engage in intellectual discussions and form connections based on shared passions for learning.

8. Explore Intergenerational Connections: Seek opportunities to engage with individuals from different age groups. Volunteer at schools or community centers that involve young people, or participate in intergenerational programs that promote meaningful interactions between older adults and younger generations.

9. Plan Social Outings: Organize social outings with friends or acquaintances, such as going to a movie, having a picnic, or taking a day trip to explore a nearby town or city. These outings create opportunities for shared experiences and strengthen bonds.

10. Foster Emotional Support Networks: Surround yourself with individuals who provide emotional support and understanding. Seek out friends or support groups that can offer a listening ear, guidance, and encouragement during both joyful and challenging times.

11. Be Open to New Connections: Stay open to forming new connections and friendships. Approach social situations with a sense of curiosity and a willingness to meet new people. Embrace diversity and appreciate the unique perspectives and experiences that each individual brings.

Cultivating meaningful connections in retirement is vital for overall well-being and a sense of belonging. By fostering social engagement, you can create a supportive network, find fulfillment in shared experiences, and enhance your overall quality of life.

"The wise planner doesn't just count the days to retirement but makes each day count toward a secure future." - Anonymous

9

EMBRACING NEW EXPERIENCES

Retirement is the perfect time to embrace new experiences and embark on exciting adventures. In this chapter, we will explore the importance of stepping out of your comfort zone and discovering the joy of trying new things during retirement.

1. Travel and Explore: Retirement offers the freedom to travel and explore new destinations. Whether it's visiting exotic locations, exploring different cultures, or immersing yourself in nature, travel can provide a sense of adventure and discovery. Plan trips that align with your interests and create memories that will last a lifetime.

2. Try a New Hobby: Retirement is the perfect time to indulge in hobbies or activities that you've always wanted to try. Whether it's painting, gardening, photography, cooking, or learning a musical instrument, pursuing new hobbies can bring a sense of fulfillment and open up new avenues of creativity.

3. Engage in Physical Activities: Stay active and maintain good health by engaging in physical activities that you enjoy. Try activities such as hiking, swimming, yoga, or dancing. Not only will these activities keep you fit, but they will also provide opportunities to meet like-minded individuals and make new friends.

4. Learn a New Skill: Challenge yourself by learning a new skill or taking up a new craft. It could be anything from woodworking to knitting, from learning a new language to mastering a new technology. The process of acquiring new skills keeps the mind sharp and opens up possibilities for personal growth.

5. Volunteer for Adventure-Based Initiatives: Look for volunteer opportunities that involve adventure or outdoor activities. Organizations such as Habitat for Humanity, wildlife conservation projects, or disaster relief initiatives often offer opportunities to engage in physically demanding work while making a positive impact.

6. Explore Your Creativity: Retirement is the perfect time to explore your creative side. Engage in activities such as writing, painting, photography, or any other form of artistic expression that sparks your interest. Allow your creativity to flow freely and discover hidden talents that you may not have had the time to explore before.

7. Join a Club or Group: Seek out clubs or groups that align with your interests and passions. Whether it's a hiking club, a photography group, or a writing circle, joining these communities will not only provide opportunities for new experiences but also foster connections with individuals who share similar interests.

 Retire with Confidence

8. Attend Workshops or Retreats: Look for workshops or retreats that focus on personal growth, wellness, or spiritual development. These immersive experiences provide an opportunity to learn, reflect, and connect with others who are on a similar journey of self-discovery.

9. Embrace Cultural Activities: Explore the rich cultural offerings in your community. Attend theater performances, art exhibitions, music concerts, or dance recitals. Immerse yourself in the beauty of different art forms and appreciate the creativity and talent of others.

10. Connect with Nature: Spend time in nature and embrace its wonders. Whether it's hiking in the mountains, walking along the beach, or simply enjoying a picnic in the park, connecting with nature can bring a sense of peace, rejuvenation, and awe-inspiring experiences.

Retirement is a time to embrace new experiences and embark on adventures that enrich your life. By stepping out of your comfort zone and trying new things, you can create a retirement filled with excitement, growth, and fulfillment.

"Build your retirement dreams with the bricks of prudence, the mortar of discipline, and the roof of financial foresight." – Anonymous

10

FINDING PURPOSE AND MEANING

Retirement is an opportunity to discover a new sense of purpose and meaning in life. In this chapter, we will explore the importance of finding meaning in retirement and ways you can create a fulfilling and purpose-driven retirement journey.

1. Reflect on Your Values and Passions: Take the time to reflect on your core values and passions. What truly matters to you in life? What activities bring you joy and fulfillment? Identifying these aspects will help guide you in finding purpose and meaning in retirement.

2. Set Meaningful Goals: Set goals that align with your values and passions. These goals can be personal, professional, or even centered around giving back to the community. Having clear goals to work towards will provide a sense of purpose and direction in your retirement journey.

 Retire with Confidence

3. Volunteer and Give Back: Engage in volunteer work that resonates with your interests and values. Whether it's supporting a cause you care about, mentoring others, or contributing your skills and expertise to a nonprofit organization, giving back can provide a deep sense of purpose and fulfillment.

4. Start a Second Career or Business: Retirement doesn't necessarily mean the end of your professional journey. Consider starting a second career or a small business in a field that ignites your passion. This can provide a renewed sense of purpose, intellectual stimulation, and the opportunity to make a meaningful impact.

5. Engage in Mentoring and Teaching: Share your knowledge and experiences with others by becoming a mentor or teacher. Offer guidance and support to younger generations or individuals who are starting out in their careers. Mentoring and teaching can be incredibly rewarding and allow you to leave a lasting impact.

6. Pursue Personal Growth: Continuously invest in your personal growth and development. Attend workshops, seminars, or conferences to expand your knowledge and skills. Engaging in lifelong learning keeps your mind sharp, fosters personal growth, and provides a sense of accomplishment.

7. Cultivate Meaningful Relationships: Surround yourself with individuals who uplift and inspire you. Build deep and meaningful relationships with family, friends, and like-minded individuals. These connections provide support, love, and a sense of belonging, enhancing your overall well-being and sense of purpose.

8. Engage in Philanthropy: Consider philanthropic activities that align with your values and passions. Support causes or organizations that are close to your heart through donations or by actively participating in fundraising events. Contributing to the greater good can bring a profound sense of fulfillment and purpose.

9. Embrace a Healthy Lifestyle: Taking care of your physical and mental well-being is essential for finding purpose and meaning in retirement. Prioritize regular exercise, eat a balanced diet, get enough sleep, and engage in activities that promote mental and emotional well-being, such as meditation or journaling.

10. Embrace Self-Reflection and Gratitude: Take time for self-reflection and gratitude. Reflect on the experiences, lessons, and achievements throughout your life, and express gratitude for the blessings and opportunities that retirement brings. Cultivating an attitude of gratitude can bring a sense of contentment and fulfillment.

Finding purpose and meaning in retirement is a personal journey that requires self-reflection and exploration. By aligning your activities with your values, passions, and goals, you can create a retirement that is truly fulfilling and purpose-driven.

"Retirement isn't the end but a new beginning paved with the wisdom of financial foresight." - Unknown

11

MAINTAINING A HEALTHY AND BALANCED LIFESTYLE IN RETIREMENT

Retirement is a time to prioritize your health and well-being. In this chapter, we will explore the importance of maintaining a healthy and balanced lifestyle in retirement and provide practical tips to help you achieve optimal physical, mental, and emotional well-being.

1. Prioritize Physical Activity: Engage in regular physical activity to stay fit and maintain your overall health. Choose activities that you enjoy, such as walking, swimming, cycling, or yoga. Aim for at least 30 minutes of moderate-intensity exercise on most days of the week. Physical activity not only improves your physical health but also boosts your mood and mental well-being.

2. Eat a Nutritious Diet: Pay attention to your diet and consume a balanced and nutritious meal. Include plenty of fruits, vegetables, whole grains, lean proteins, and healthy fats in your diet. Limit processed foods, sugary snacks, and excessive amounts of salt and saturated fats.

A healthy diet provides the necessary nutrients to support your overall health and energy levels.

3. Get Enough Sleep: Prioritize getting an adequate amount of sleep each night. Aim for 7-8 hours of quality sleep to allow your body to rest, repair, and rejuvenate. Establish a bedtime routine and create a sleep-friendly environment to promote better sleep quality.

4. Foster Social Connections: Maintain and cultivate social connections in retirement. Spend time with family and friends, join community groups, or participate in social activities that align with your interests. Social connections provide a sense of belonging, support, and overall well-being.

5. Engage in Intellectual Stimulation: Keep your mind sharp and engaged by engaging in intellectually stimulating activities. Read books, solve puzzles, play strategy games, or take up new hobbies that challenge your cognitive abilities. Continuous mental stimulation helps maintain cognitive function and prevents cognitive decline.

6. Manage Stress: Retirement may come with its own set of stressors. Find healthy ways to manage stress, such as practicing relaxation techniques, meditation, deep breathing exercises, or engaging in activities that bring you joy and help you unwind. Prioritize self-care and take time for yourself to recharge and rejuvenate.

7. Stay Connected with Healthcare: Regularly visit your healthcare providers for check-ups, screenings, and preventive care. Stay up-to-date with vaccinations and screenings appropriate for your age and health conditions. Maintain open communication with your healthcare team and address any health concerns promptly.

8. Embrace Technology: Embrace technology to stay connected, learn new skills, and access health information. Use smartphones, tablets, or computers to communicate with loved ones, engage in online courses or webinars, and access health-related resources. Technology can enhance your retirement experience and keep you connected to the world.

9. Practice Mindfulness: Incorporate mindfulness practices into your daily routine. Take moments to pause, breathe, and be present in the current moment. Mindfulness can help reduce stress, improve focus, and enhance overall well-being.

10. Embrace Leisure and Recreation: Make time for leisure and recreational activities that bring you joy and relaxation. Engage in hobbies, pursue interests, or simply take time to enjoy nature and engage in activities that bring you a sense of pleasure and fulfillment.

By prioritizing your health and well-being in retirement, you can enjoy a fulfilling and balanced lifestyle. Remember to listen to your body, take care of your mental and emotional needs, and make choices that support your overall well-being.

> *"Cultivate the seeds of financial prudence in the garden of life for a fruitful retirement." - Anonymous*

12

MAINTAINING MEANINGFUL RELATIONSHIPS AND CONNECTIONS IN RETIREMENT

Retirement is an opportune time to cultivate and strengthen meaningful relationships. In this chapter, we will explore the importance of maintaining connections with loved ones and building new relationships in retirement. We'll also provide practical tips on how to nurture these relationships for a fulfilling retirement experience.

1. Prioritize Communication: Communication is key to maintaining meaningful relationships. Stay connected with loved ones through regular phone calls, video chats, or in-person visits. Share updates, stories, and experiences to keep the connection alive and vibrant.

2. Engage in Shared Activities: Participate in shared activities with your loved ones. Plan outings, vacations, or hobbies that you can enjoy together. Engaging in shared experiences strengthens the bond and creates lasting memories.

3. Join Social and Community Groups: Explore social and community groups that align with your interests and values. Join clubs, organizations, or volunteer groups where you can meet like-minded individuals. These groups provide opportunities to form new connections and expand your social circle.

4. Attend Social Events and Gatherings: Attend social events, parties, or gatherings in your community. Engaging in these activities allows you to interact with different people and fosters a sense of belonging within your community.

5. Foster Intergenerational Relationships: Seek opportunities to connect with individuals from different generations. Interact with younger family members, participate in mentorship programs, or volunteer at schools or youth organizations. Building intergenerational relationships brings new perspectives, shared wisdom, and a sense of purpose.

6. Be a Good Listener: Actively listen to others when engaging in conversations. Show genuine interest and empathy in their stories, experiences, and feelings. Being a good listener strengthens relationships and creates a safe and supportive environment.

7. Practice Empathy and Understanding: Cultivate empathy and understanding in your relationships. Put yourself in the other person's shoes and try to see things from their perspective. This fosters a deeper connection and enhances the quality of your relationships.

 Retire with Confidence

8. Resolve Conflicts with Open Communication: Conflict is a natural part of any relationship. When conflicts arise, approach them with open communication and a willingness to find a resolution. Address concerns, listen to each other's viewpoints, and work together to find common ground.

9. Plan Regular Gatherings: Organize regular gatherings or reunions with family and friends. These events provide an opportunity to reconnect, strengthen bonds, and create cherished memories.

10. Embrace Technology for Connection: Utilize technology to stay connected with loved ones who may be far away. Video calls, social media, and messaging apps can bridge the distance and maintain the connection.

11. Seek Support and Companionship: If you're feeling lonely or isolated, seek support and companionship. Join support groups, seek therapy if needed, or consider adopting a pet. Having a support system can provide comfort, companionship, and a sense of belonging.

12. Cultivate Friendships with Shared Interests: Seek out individuals who share your interests and hobbies. Join clubs, classes, or online communities centered around your passions. Building friendships with individuals who share your interests can lead to fulfilling and meaningful connections.

13. Show Appreciation and Gratitude: Express gratitude and appreciation for the people in your life. Let them know how much they mean to you and how grateful you are for their presence. Small acts of kindness and appreciation go a long way in nurturing relationships.

14. Be Open to New Connections: Be open to forming new connections and friendships in retirement. Embrace opportunities to meet new people, engage in new activities, and be receptive to the potential for new meaningful relationships.

15. Invest Time and Effort: Building and maintaining meaningful relationships requires time and effort. Prioritize your relationships by dedicating time to nurture them. Schedule regular meetups, phone calls, or outings to stay connected.

By prioritizing and nurturing your relationships, you can create a rich and fulfilling retirement experience. Meaningful connections bring joy, support, and a sense of belonging. In the next chapter, we will explore the topic of embracing new adventures and experiences in retirement. Join us as we continue our journey toward a fulfilling retirement.

"Craft your retirement nest egg with the patience of a sculptor, creating a masterpiece for your golden years." - Anonymous

13

EMBRACING NEW ADVENTURES AND EXPERIENCES IN RETIREMENT

Retirement is a time of freedom and exploration. In this chapter, we will delve into the importance of embracing new adventures and experiences in retirement. We'll discuss the benefits of stepping out of your comfort zone, provide practical tips for trying new things, and inspire you to make the most of this exciting chapter in your life.

1. Embrace a Growth Mindset: Adopt a growth mindset that encourages you to seek out new experiences and challenges. Believe in your ability to learn and adapt, and view each opportunity as a chance for personal growth and enrichment.

2. Step Out of Your Comfort Zone: Break free from the familiar and venture into new territories. Try activities or hobbies that you've always been curious about but never had the time or opportunity to pursue. Stepping out of your comfort zone can lead to personal discovery and a renewed sense of excitement.

3. Travel and Explore: Explore new destinations near and far. Travel allows you to immerse yourself in different cultures, experience new cuisines, and discover breathtaking landscapes. Whether you prefer solo travel, group tours, or RV adventures, there is a world waiting to be explored.

4. Learn Something New: Engage in lifelong learning by acquiring new skills or knowledge. Enroll in classes, workshops, or online courses that align with your interests. Whether it's learning a musical instrument, painting, cooking, or a new language, the process of learning keeps the mind sharp and opens doors to new possibilities.

5. Volunteer and Give Back: Dedicate your time and skills to meaningful causes or organizations. Volunteering provides an opportunity to make a positive impact, meet new people, and gain a sense of fulfillment. Choose a cause that resonates with you and contribute in a way that aligns with your skills and interests.

6. Engage in Creative Pursuits: Tap into your creativity by exploring artistic pursuits. Paint, write, dance, or play music to express yourself and unleash your inner artist. Engaging in creative activities can be a source of joy, self-expression, and personal growth.

7. Try New Sports or Physical Activities: Engage in physical activities or sports that you've never tried before. Join a local sports club, take up hiking, golfing, or even try out adventurous activities like rock climbing or kayaking. Physical activity not only improves your health but also boosts your confidence and sense of achievement.

    Retire with Confidence

8. Attend Workshops and Retreats: Attend workshops or retreats that focus on personal growth, wellness, or mindfulness. These immersive experiences provide an opportunity to learn, reflect, and connect with like-minded individuals who share similar interests and passions.

9. Become an Entrepreneur: If you've always had a business idea or dreamt of starting your own venture, retirement can be the perfect time to pursue it. Consider turning your passion into a small business or consultancy. Entrepreneurship can be a fulfilling and rewarding endeavor that allows you to share your expertise and make a difference.

10. Connect with Nature: Spend time in nature and embrace outdoor activities. Whether it's gardening, hiking, birdwatching, or simply enjoying a picnic in the park, immersing yourself in nature can have a calming and rejuvenating effect on your mind, body, and spirit.

11. Foster Cultural Appreciation: Immerse yourself in different cultures through art, music, literature, or cuisine. Visit museums, attend cultural festivals, explore different cuisines, or read books from around the world. Embracing different cultures expands your horizons and deepens your understanding of the world.

12. Document Your Adventures: Keep a journal, start a blog, or create a photo album to document your retirement adventures. Capture the memories and reflections of your experiences to cherish and share with loved ones. It's a wonderful way to preserve your legacy and inspire others.

13. Join Social Clubs or Groups: Join social clubs or groups that align with your interests and passions. Whether it's a book club, hiking group, or a hobby-specific community, these clubs provide opportunities to meet like-minded individuals and share experiences.

14. Attend Cultural Events and Performances: Immerse yourself in the arts by attending theater performances, concerts, art exhibitions, or poetry readings. Cultural events offer a chance to appreciate creativity and immerse yourself in the beauty of artistic expression.

15. Embrace Spontaneity: Allow yourself to be spontaneous and open to new opportunities that arise. Say yes to invitations, take unplanned road trips, or try spur-of-the-moment activities. Embracing spontaneity adds an element of excitement and unpredictability to your retirement journey.

Embracing new adventures and experiences in retirement can bring a renewed sense of purpose, joy, and vitality. Stay open to the possibilities, step out of your comfort zone, and embrace the richness that this chapter of life has to offer.

In the next and final chapter, we will reflect on the journey so far and offer guidance on leaving a lasting legacy. Join us as we conclude our journey toward a fulfilling retirement

"A well-planned retirement is the symphony of a lifetime's financial harmony." - Unknown

14

LEAVING A LASTING LEGACY

As we near the end of our journey toward a fulfilling retirement, it's essential to reflect on the legacy we want to leave behind. We will explore the concept of leaving a lasting legacy and provide guidance on how to make a positive impact on future generations.

Let's delve into the significance of legacy and discover practical ways to create a meaningful and enduring impact.

1. Define Your Values and Beliefs: Start by reflecting on your core values and beliefs. What principles have guided your life? What do you hold dear? Understanding your values will help shape your legacy and ensure that it aligns with who you are as an individual.

2. Identify Your Passions and Talents: Consider your passions and talents. What activities or causes have brought you the most joy and fulfillment throughout your life? Identifying these passions and talents will allow you to focus your energy on areas where you can make the greatest impact.

 Retire with Confidence

3. Share Your Wisdom and Knowledge: One of the most valuable contributions you can make is sharing your wisdom and knowledge with others. Consider mentoring younger individuals, teaching, or writing a book to pass on your experiences and insights. Your knowledge can inspire and guide future generations.

4. Engage in Philanthropy: Philanthropy is an excellent way to leave a lasting impact. Identify causes or organizations that resonate with your values and support them through donations, volunteering, or even establishing a charitable foundation. Philanthropy allows you to make a positive difference in areas close to your heart.

5. Create a Family Legacy: Leaving a legacy within your family is equally important. Share family stories, traditions, and values with younger generations. Foster strong relationships and create a sense of connection that will endure for years to come.

6. Preserve Your Family History: Take the time to preserve your family history and genealogy. Gather photographs, documents, and stories that tell the story of your family's past. This not only creates a sense of identity for future generations but also preserves their heritage.

7. Volunteer and Give Back: Engage in volunteer work that aligns with your passions and interests. Whether it's supporting a local community organization, working with a nonprofit, or helping those in need, volunteering allows you to make a positive impact and leave a legacy of compassion and service.

8. Be an Environmental Steward: Consider the impact you have on the environment and strive to be an environmental steward. Adopt sustainable practices, reduce waste, and support initiatives that promote conservation and environmental protection. Leaving a healthy planet for future generations is a powerful legacy.

9. Mentor and Inspire Others: Offer your guidance and support to individuals who can benefit from your experience and expertise. Mentorship can be formal or informal and can occur in various areas of life, such as career, personal development, or specific skills. Mentoring others allows you to leave a lasting impact on their lives.

10. Document Your Legacy: Consider creating a personal legacy document that outlines your values, beliefs, and the impact you want to have. This document can serve as a guide for future generations and ensure that your legacy is carried forward according to your wishes.

11. Support Education and Learning: Education is the key to progress and development. Support educational initiatives by sponsoring scholarships, donating to educational institutions, or starting educational programs. By investing in education, you contribute to the growth and development of future generations.

12. Foster Positive Relationships: Cultivate meaningful relationships and connections with those around you. Be a source of support, love, and encouragement to your family, friends, and community. Leaving a legacy of strong relationships and positive connections is invaluable.

13. Live Your Values: Ultimately, the most impactful way to leave a lasting legacy is to live your life in accordance with your values. Set the example and allow your actions to convey more than words ever could. Be kind, compassionate, and authentic in everything you do, leaving a positive imprint on the world.

14. Share Your Story: Consider sharing your own life story with others. Write a memoir, record your experiences, or participate in storytelling events. Your story has the power to inspire, motivate, and provide valuable lessons to future generations.

15. Be Remembered for Love and Kindness: Above all, strive to be remembered for the love and kindness you showed to others. Leave behind a legacy of compassion, empathy, and a genuine care for humanity. By leaving a positive impact on the lives of others, you create a legacy that will endure for generations to come.

As we conclude our journey toward a fulfilling retirement, remember that the legacy you leave behind is a testament to the life you have lived and the impact you have made.

Embrace the opportunity to create a lasting legacy that reflects your values, passions, and the love you have shared with others. May your legacy inspire and guide future generations to live purposeful and meaningful lives.

"In the tapestry of life, weave
the threads of financial
wisdom for a retirement rich
in fulfillment." - Unknown

CONCLUSION

As you reach the final chapter of "Retire with Confidence: A Comprehensive Guide to Financial Security and Fulfillment," envision the canvas of your future unfurling before you. The brushstrokes of your financial choices and life decisions have painted a portrait of retirement that is uniquely yours.

In concluding our journey together, remember that retirement is not just a destination but a dynamic chapter in the grand story of your life. The knowledge and insights gathered throughout this guide are not mere tools; they are the compass guiding you toward a retirement imbued with both security and fulfillment.

Your financial well-being is a cornerstone, but true confidence in retirement springs from the balance of financial prudence, personal fulfillment, and meaningful connections. As you embark on this new phase, consider each challenge as an opportunity to showcase the resilience that has been the hallmark of your entire journey.

Your retirement is an evolving masterpiece, shaped by the wisdom you've acquired, the dreams you've pursued, and the relationships you've cherished. It's a symphony of experiences, accomplishments, and the joy derived from a life well-lived.

Embrace the adventure that retirement offers—a time to explore, create, give back, and revel in the simple pleasures. Let your newfound freedom be the stage for the encore of your passions and the discovery of new ones.

 Retire with Confidence

As you bid farewell to the working world, do so not with trepidation, but with the confidence that comes from thoughtful planning, a diversified approach to investments, and a holistic view of your well-being. Your retirement is an unfolding narrative, and each day is a blank page waiting to be filled with the richness of your experiences.

May your retirement be a chapter filled with the laughter of shared moments, the warmth of cherished relationships, and the satisfaction of a life lived on your terms. Your financial security is the foundation, but the true legacy of your retirement will be the impact you make on the world around you.

In closing, may this guide be a compass, a source of inspiration, and a companion on your journey toward retirement that radiates confidence and fulfillment. As you step into this new chapter, remember that you have the power to sculpt a retirement that reflects the very essence of who you are and what you aspire to be.

Here's to your retirement—a canvas waiting for the strokes of your unique and extraordinary story!

 Retire with Confidence